CONTENTS

VALUATION VS. PROFITABILITY

THE STARTUP DILEMMA

13 THINGS EVERY STARTUP FOUNDER
MUST KEEP IN MIND

VIKAS DEVNANI

INDIA • SINGAPORE • MALAYSIA

Copyright © Vikas Devnani 2025

All Rights Reserved.

ISBN

Paperback 979-8-89906-800-3

Hardcase 979-8-89961-893-2

The Startup Dilemma – Valuation vs. Profitability

Why This Book Matters

Every founder dreams of building the next big thing—**a company that changes the world and creates massive wealth.**

But there's a **fundamental question** every startup must answer early on:

Should we focus on increasing valuation or achieving profitability?

This single decision determines:

- ✓ How you **fund your startup.**
- ✓ Whether you **prioritize growth or sustainability.**
- ✓ The kind of **investors you attract.**
- ✓ When and how you **exit the company.**

Many of the biggest startups—**Amazon, Uber, and Airbnb**—chose **valuation-first** strategies, raising billions before turning a profit.

Others—**Mailchimp, Basecamp, and Patagonia**—focused on **profitability from day one**, avoiding external funding and building sustainable businesses.

Both approaches have created **massive successes**—and **huge failures.**

So, how do you decide **which path is right for your startup?**

The Founder's Dilemma

Imagine you're the founder of a **fast-growing startup.**

You have two choices:

Path 1: The Valuation-First Strategy

- You **raise millions** in venture capital.

- You **spend aggressively** to scale—hiring, marketing, expanding.

- Your company is **growing fast**, but you're burning cash.

- Investors push you for **more growth**, even if you're not making a profit.

🔨 **Potential Outcome:**

✓ If successful, you become a **unicorn ($1B+ valuation)** and go public.

✗ If unsuccessful, you **run out of funding** and collapse.

Path 2: The Profitability-First Strategy

- You **focus on revenue & sustainability**.

- You **grow steadily**, but at a **slower pace**.

- You **don't rely on VC funding**, maintaining control.

- You **generate profit early**, making the business self-sufficient.

🔨 **Potential Outcome:**

✓ If successful, you build a **long-lasting company** with financial stability.

✗ If unsuccessful, you struggle to **scale fast enough** and miss market opportunities.

What This Book Will Teach You

This book will help you answer:

☑ **When to prioritize valuation vs. profitability.**

☑ **How to attract investors while keeping financial control.**

☑ **Which business models work best for each strategy.**

☑ **How to scale smartly without burning out.**

☑ **Real-life case studies of startups that succeeded—and failed—using both approaches.**

Who This Book Is For

This book is for:

- **Startup founders** deciding how to scale.
- **Entrepreneurs** looking to raise funding or bootstrap.
- **Investors** evaluating growth strategies.
- **Business students** learning about startup economics.

Whether you're launching, scaling, or planning your exit, this book will give you **the knowledge to make the right decisions** for your startup.

Let's dive in and explore the **battle between valuation and profitability**—and how you can navigate it to build a successful business.

CHAPTER 1

THE GREAT DEBATE

Every startup founder faces a fundamental question: **Should I focus on increasing my company's valuation or work towards profitability?**

Some of the biggest tech companies today, like Amazon, Tesla, and Uber, spent years prioritizing growth and valuation, raising billions from investors while burning cash. Others, like Basecamp and Mailchimp, rejected venture capital and focused entirely on profits from day one. Both approaches have created massive successes—and notable failures.

But which one is right for your startup?

Valuation vs. Profitability: What's the Difference?

Before diving into real-world examples, let's clarify these two concepts:

- **Valuation** is the estimated worth of a company based on investments, future potential, and market conditions. Startups that prioritize valuation often raise significant funding rounds and reinvest the capital into growth, even at the expense of profitability.

- **Profitability** means that a company earns more revenue than it spends. Profit-driven startups focus on making money from customers rather than relying on investors.

At first glance, the choice might seem obvious—why wouldn't every company aim for profitability? But the reality is more complicated.

The Case for Valuation: The Growth-at-All-Costs Model

Imagine two founders launching competing food delivery startups in a new city. One founder bootstraps, growing slowly through word-of-mouth and organic sales. The other raises $100 million in venture capital and immediately offers discounts, free deliveries, and aggressive marketing.

Which startup is likely to win?

History suggests that the latter often dominates the market—at least in the short term. By focusing on valuation and rapid growth, companies can:

- **Scale quickly and dominate an industry.** Amazon operated at a loss for years, prioritizing growth over profits to become the world's largest retailer.

- **Attract top talent and investors.** Higher valuations bring in top-tier employees and more investment capital.

- **Outcompete slower-moving rivals.** Uber, despite massive losses, crushed local competitors with aggressive expansion and discounts.

However, chasing valuation comes with risks. Companies like WeWork and Theranos collapsed after inflating their worth without sustainable business models.

The Case for Profitability: The Sustainable Approach

On the other end of the spectrum, some startups refuse outside funding and focus solely on making money. Companies like **Basecamp** and **Mailchimp** rejected venture capital and grew profitably from the beginning.

- **Basecamp**, a project management software company, built a multimillion-dollar business without raising money. The founders controlled their destiny, focusing on long-term stability rather than chasing investors.

- **Mailchimp**, an email marketing platform, bootstrapped to a $12 billion valuation before being acquired—without ever taking venture capital.

Profitability-focused startups benefit from:

- **Financial independence.** Without investors, founders retain full control over decision-making.

- **Resilience in downturns.** Profit-making companies survive economic downturns better than unprofitable startups.

- **Long-term stability.** While growth is slower, profitable startups avoid the risk of burning out.

But this approach has challenges. Without external funding, these companies may struggle to scale quickly or compete against venture-backed rivals.

So, What's the Right Approach?

The reality is that both strategies can work—but not in every situation. Some industries (like AI or biotech) require massive upfront investment, making profitability difficult in the early years. Others (like SaaS or e-commerce) can grow profitably from day one.

Over the next chapters, we'll dive deeper into real-world examples of startups that succeeded—and failed—on both paths. By the end of this book, you'll have a clear framework for deciding which approach is best for your startup.

CHAPTER 2

THE STARTUP LIFECYCLE – FROM IDEA TO SCALE

Before deciding whether to focus on valuation or profitability, startup founders must understand how priorities shift across different stages of a company's growth. A pre-revenue startup raising its first round of funding has vastly different challenges than a company preparing for an IPO.

The Four Stages of a Startup

Most startups progress through the following lifecycle:

1. **Idea & Early Validation (Pre-Seed & Seed Stage)**

2. **Growth & Market Expansion (Series A-C)**

3. **Scaling & Maturity (Late-Stage Funding & Pre-IPO)**

4. **Sustained Profitability or Exit (IPO, Acquisition, or Long-Term Operation)**

Each stage presents unique opportunities and challenges in balancing valuation and profitability.

1. **Idea & Early Validation: The MVP Stage**

    At this stage, startups are focused on **validating their idea** with a minimum viable product (MVP). Founders typically rely on **personal savings, angel investors, or early-stage VCs** to fund operations.

    Real-World Example: Airbnb's Early Hustle

    In 2008, Airbnb was far from a billion-dollar company. Founders Brian Chesky and Joe Gebbia struggled to gain traction, so they launched an unconventional strategy: they sold **custom-designed cereal boxes**

("Obama O's" and "Cap'n McCain's") to fund their business. This early move kept Airbnb afloat before raising serious venture capital.

At this stage, valuation is often **more important than profitability**. Startups need funding to build their product, acquire initial users, and iterate based on feedback.

2. **Growth & Market Expansion: Scaling Up**

Once a startup has validated its idea and gained early customers, the focus shifts to **growth**. This is where startups typically raise **Series A, B, or C rounds**, often prioritizing market share over immediate profitability.

Real-World Example: Amazon's Relentless Growth

Jeff Bezos famously told investors that Amazon wouldn't focus on profits in its early years. Instead, the company reinvested revenue into growth—expanding its product lines, building infrastructure, and acquiring customers. This strategy led Amazon to dominate e-commerce, even though it was unprofitable for years.

Many VCs prefer startups to focus on **scaling quickly** rather than making money immediately. Why? Because in competitive markets, **the winner often takes all**.

But this approach has risks. Companies that focus **too much** on valuation can overextend themselves.

Real-World Example: WeWork's Overinflated Valuation

WeWork, once valued at **$47 billion**, aggressively expanded without a clear path to profitability. The company burned billions on office leases, assuming continuous growth. When investors questioned its financials, its valuation collapsed, and the IPO was canceled.

Lesson? **Growth is essential, but reckless spending can backfire.**

3. **Scaling & Maturity: Finding the Balance**

As startups reach late-stage funding rounds or approach an IPO, profitability becomes more critical. Investors begin demanding **clear revenue models** and a path to positive cash flow.

Real-World Example: Facebook's Monetization Strategy

For years, Facebook focused purely on user growth, avoiding aggressive monetization. But as it matured, it introduced targeted advertising, transforming it into a **profit-making machine**.

At this stage, startups must decide whether to:

- **Prepare for IPO** (like Uber and Airbnb)

- **Pursue acquisition** (like WhatsApp and Instagram)

- **Operate as a sustainable, profitable business** (like Atlassian and Basecamp)

4. **Sustained Profitability or Exit**

At this point, a startup must become **self-sustaining**. Investors expect consistent revenue, and the company either:

- Becomes **publicly traded** (like Google and Tesla)

- Gets **acquired** (like YouTube and LinkedIn)

- Remains **private but profitable** (like SpaceX and Stripe)

Real-World Example: Shopify's Steady Growth

Unlike many tech startups that prioritized valuation, Shopify built a sustainable business early on. By focusing on a **strong business model**, it became **profitable while still growing fast**.

Key Takeaways: When to Prioritize Valuation vs. Profitability

- **Early-stage startups** → Focus on valuation (raise funds, build product).

- **Growth-stage startups** → Scale aggressively but manage spending.

- **Late-stage startups** → Transition toward profitability.

- **Mature companies** → Prioritize sustained profitability or prepare for exit.

Understanding where your startup is in this lifecycle can help you decide whether to chase valuation or build a profitable business.

CHAPTER 3

THE POWER OF STORYTELLING IN RAISING VALUATION

Introduction: Why Storytelling Matters in Startups

Imagine two founders pitching their startups to investors.

- The first founder gives a detailed breakdown of financials, market size, and business operations.

- The second founder tells a compelling story—painting a vision of how their startup will change the world.

Who do you think raises more money?

The answer is **almost always the storyteller**.

While numbers matter, the ability to **craft a compelling narrative** plays a massive role in determining a startup's valuation. Investors don't just fund businesses; they fund **visions of the future**.

How Storytelling Creates Billion-Dollar Valuations

Many of the world's most valuable startups were built on powerful narratives that captivated investors, customers, and employees.

1. **Tesla: The Story of a Better Future**

   In the early 2000s, electric cars were seen as slow, unattractive, and impractical. But Elon Musk didn't just pitch an electric vehicle company— he told a story about **revolutionizing the world's transportation and energy systems**.

- Tesla's valuation soared despite years of losses because investors bought into **Musk's vision of a sustainable future.**

- Even as Tesla burned cash, its stock price skyrocketed because people believed it was **more than just a car company**—it was an energy revolution.

Lesson? **A powerful story can make investors overlook short-term losses in favor of long-term potential.**

2. **Airbnb: More Than Just Renting Rooms**

When Airbnb launched, the idea of **staying in a stranger's home** sounded absurd. But the founders didn't pitch it as a hotel alternative; they framed it as **a way to experience cities like a local.**

- Their story? **"Belong Anywhere"**—a vision of a world where people could feel at home no matter where they traveled.

- Investors weren't just backing a booking platform; they were investing in **a new way of travel.**

By 2020, Airbnb's IPO valuation hit **$100 billion**, despite losing **$4.6 billion** that year.

3. **Uber: The Narrative of Convenience & Disruption**

Uber didn't sell investors on just a ride-hailing app. Its founders told a story of **eliminating car ownership, reducing traffic, and democratizing transportation**.

- Investors poured billions into Uber, not because of immediate profitability, but because they believed in the **vision of global transportation dominance.**

- At its IPO in 2019, Uber was valued at **$82 billion**, despite never turning a profit.

The Three Pillars of a Strong Startup Story

If you're a founder aiming to raise money and increase your startup's valuation, your storytelling should include three key elements:

1. **A Big, Bold Vision**

Investors love big markets and ambitious founders. If your startup is solving a **massive problem** or disrupting a traditional industry, highlight that.

Example: SpaceX wasn't just about launching rockets—it was about making humans a **multi-planetary species**.

2. **A Clear Hero (Your Startup) vs. a Villain (The Problem You Solve)**

Great stories have a **hero** (your startup) fighting a **villain** (an outdated system, inefficiency, or major problem).

Example: Robinhood's story wasn't just about stock trading—it was about **fighting against Wall Street's elite and empowering everyday investors**.

3. **Proof That Your Vision is Achievable**

A great story needs credibility. Show traction, real-world impact, and a path to execution.

Example: Netflix's pitch wasn't just about beating Blockbuster—it showed how streaming would replace physical media.

Can Storytelling Go Too Far? The WeWork & Theranos Collapse

While storytelling can boost a startup's valuation, it can also lead to **overhyped failures**.

WeWork: The $47 Billion Illusion

Adam Neumann convinced investors that WeWork wasn't just a real estate company—it was a **tech-driven movement** reshaping the way people worked.

- Investors bought the vision, pushing its valuation to **$47 billion**.

- The problem? **WeWork was fundamentally a real estate company with huge losses.**

- When investors realized the numbers didn't match the story, the IPO collapsed, and the valuation plunged to **under $10 billion**.

Theranos: The Most Infamous Startup Scam

Elizabeth Holmes raised **$700 million** for Theranos by telling a story about **revolutionizing blood testing**.

- The vision? A small device that could detect diseases from a single drop of blood.

- The problem? The technology **never worked**.

- Once exposed, Theranos collapsed, and Holmes was convicted of fraud.

Balancing Storytelling with Real Growth

For founders, the key lesson is this: **A great story can raise money, but only real execution builds a lasting business.**

- **Valuation-driven startups** → Need strong storytelling to attract funding.

- **Profitability-driven startups** → Use storytelling to differentiate and attract customers.

The best companies master both. **They inspire investors with their vision but back it up with real results.**

In the next chapter, we'll explore **how venture capital influences the "growth-at-all-costs" mindset—and when startups should embrace or resist it.**

Chapter 4

Venture Capital and Growth at All Costs

Introduction: The VC Mindset

Venture capital (VC) is often seen as the fuel that powers high-growth startups. But with VC funding comes a **growth-at-all-costs** mentality—one that prioritizes **market dominance over profitability**.

For many startups, VC funding is essential for survival and scale. But for others, chasing high valuations can lead to unsustainable business models.

In this chapter, we'll explore:

- Why VCs prioritize **growth over profits**

- The **advantages** and **risks** of VC funding

- Real-world cases of startups that **thrived** (and failed) under VC pressure

Why VCs Care About Growth, Not Profitability

Most venture capital firms operate on a simple principle: **Make 10 bets, and hope 1 of them becomes a unicorn.**

VCs expect that **most startups will fail**, but they invest in **a few companies with the potential to reach billion-dollar valuations.**

- A startup growing 100% year-over-year looks attractive, even if it's losing money.

- A startup making small, steady profits but growing slowly? **Not interesting to VCs.**

This is why companies like **Uber, DoorDash, and Snapchat** raised billions while remaining unprofitable for years.

VCs don't need startups to be profitable—they need them to be valuable enough to sell (IPO or acquisition).

The Benefits of VC Funding

Many of today's biggest tech giants wouldn't exist without venture capital. **Why do startups raise VC money?**

1. **Rapid Growth & Market Domination**

   Startups with VC funding can **scale quickly**, outpacing competitors.

   - **Example: Uber vs. Local Taxis** – Uber aggressively expanded into cities, subsidizing rides with VC money to attract users. Local taxis, operating profitably but growing slowly, couldn't keep up.

2. **Hiring Top Talent & Building a Strong Team**

   VC-backed startups can afford to attract the best engineers, marketers, and executives.

   - **Example: Stripe & Google** – Stripe lured top engineers from Google and Facebook with high salaries and stock options, thanks to its VC war chest.

3. **R&D & Product Development**

   VC funding allows startups to **experiment and innovate** without immediate pressure to make money.

   - **Example: SpaceX & AI Startups** – Companies like SpaceX, OpenAI, and DeepMind required billions in funding before their technology could generate revenue.

The Risks of VC-Backed Growth

While VC funding enables massive growth, it also comes with **pressures and pitfalls.**

1. **Unsustainable Business Models**

   Many VC-funded startups **burn cash too quickly**, assuming future revenue will make up for losses.

- **Example: WeWork's Collapse** – WeWork spent billions expanding into global markets, assuming **growth alone** would justify its valuation. But when profits never came, the bubble burst.

2. **Losing Control Over Your Company**

VCs demand equity in exchange for funding, meaning founders **lose ownership and decision-making power**.

- **Example: Steve Jobs Ousted from Apple** – In 1985, Apple's board—backed by investors—fired Steve Jobs from the company he founded.

3. **The "Grow or Die" Pressure**

VCs expect **constant, aggressive growth**. If startups fail to meet high targets, they can lose funding and collapse.

- **Example: MoviePass & the $10 Subscription Model** – MoviePass offered unlimited movies for $10/month, gaining millions of users. But because their costs far outweighed revenue, the company quickly burned through cash and died.

When Should Startups Take VC Money?

While VC funding is tempting, it's not the right choice for every startup. Here's a guide:

Scenario	VC Funding is a Good Idea	VC Funding May Be Risky
Market Size	If you're in a **huge, scalable** market (e.g., AI, fintech, marketplaces).	If your market is **niche** and doesn't justify hyper-growth.
Cash Burn	If your business **requires significant upfront capital** (e.g., biotech, hardware).	If you can grow profitably without external funding.
Competitive Landscape	If you need to **move fast before competitors** take the market (e.g., ride-sharing, delivery).	If competition is low, you may not need VC speed.
Founder Goals	If you're willing to **give up control for fast growth**.	If you prefer to **retain full ownership** and scale steadily.

Case Study: Startups That Succeeded Without VC

Some companies rejected VC funding and **built profitable businesses instead**.

1. **Mailchimp: The Billion-Dollar Bootstrapper**

    - Mailchimp started as a side business and **never raised VC money**.

    - Grew profitably through customer revenue.

    - Eventually sold for **$12 billion**—with **founders keeping 100% ownership**.

2. **Basecamp: Prioritizing Profitability Over Growth**

    - Basecamp's founders refused VC funding.

    - Focused on sustainable, long-term profitability.

    - Built a successful SaaS business while keeping ownership.

3. **Zoho: Competing with Giants Without Venture Capital**

    - Zoho competes with **Microsoft and Google** in enterprise software.

    - **Zero outside investment**—funded purely by customer revenue.

    - Now generates **over $1 billion in annual revenue**.

Conclusion: Should You Chase VC or Profitability?

- If you're in a **high-growth industry (AI, fintech, marketplaces)** and need to scale quickly, **VC funding makes sense**.

- If you can build a profitable business **without giving up control**, it might be smarter to **bootstrap** and retain ownership.

- The best startups find a **balance**—raising capital when needed but staying focused on **building a real, sustainable business**.

Next Chapter: The Unicorn Dream – How Startups Achieve Billion-Dollar Valuations

In the next chapter, we'll explore how startups **become unicorns**—companies valued at **$1 billion+**—and what it takes to reach that level.

CHAPTER 5

THE UNICORN DREAM – HOW STARTUPS ACHIEVE BILLION-DOLLAR VALUATIONS

Introduction: The Pursuit of a $1 Billion Valuation

The term **"unicorn"** was coined by venture capitalist Aileen Lee in 2013 to describe **startups valued at $1 billion or more**. Back then, unicorns were rare. Today, there are over **1,200 unicorns worldwide**, including companies like Stripe, ByteDance (TikTok), and SpaceX.

But what does it take to reach a billion-dollar valuation?

In this chapter, we'll break down:

- The **common traits of unicorn startups**
- Real-world examples of how companies reached unicorn status
- The **trade-offs** founders face when chasing billion-dollar valuations

What Makes a Unicorn? The 5 Key Traits

Most unicorn startups share these five characteristics:

1. **A Massive Market Opportunity**

   Unicorns don't just serve small customer bases—they **target massive global markets.**

   - **Example: Airbnb (Hospitality Market - $3.9 Trillion)**
     - ◊ Instead of competing with hotels directly, Airbnb expanded the hospitality market by turning homes into lodging options.

- ◊ This **unlocked millions of new hosts and travelers**, fueling its valuation growth.

- ■ **Example: Robinhood (Retail Investing - $100 Trillion)**

  - ◊ Robinhood didn't just offer stock trading—it **democratized investing for young, first-time traders**.

  - ◊ This expanded the customer base beyond traditional brokerage users.

Lesson: If your market is small, reaching a billion-dollar valuation is unlikely.

2. **Disruptive Innovation & Competitive Advantage**

Unicorns don't just **improve** existing industries—they **redefine them**.

- ■ **Example: Uber (Ride-Hailing Disruption)**

  - ◊ Before Uber, getting a taxi was slow, unreliable, and expensive.

  - ◊ Uber leveraged **mobile technology + gig workers** to create a **better, faster** transportation model.

- ■ **Example: Stripe (Payments Disruption)**

  - ◊ Traditional payment systems were **complex** and required **weeks** to integrate.

  - ◊ Stripe offered **instant, developer-friendly payment APIs**, fueling e-commerce growth.

Lesson: If a startup solves **the same problem as existing players** but only slightly better, it's unlikely to be a unicorn.

3. **Explosive Growth & Network Effects**

Most unicorns grow at **insanely fast rates** and benefit from **network effects** (where each new user increases the product's value).

- ■ **Example: TikTok (Virality & Network Effects)**

  - ◊ TikTok's algorithm creates **personalized, addictive content**, making users stay longer.

  - ◊ The more users join, the **better** the recommendations, increasing growth.

- ■ **Example: WhatsApp (Zero Marketing, 2 Billion Users)**

- ◊ WhatsApp relied on **word-of-mouth virality** instead of advertising.
- ◊ As more people used WhatsApp, it became **the go-to messaging app** worldwide.

Lesson: Startups that **grow exponentially** have a higher chance of reaching unicorn status.

4. **Strong VC Backing & Capital Injection**

Most unicorns **raise massive funding rounds** to fuel their growth.

- ■ **Example: WeWork (Raised $12 Billion Pre-IPO)**
  - ◊ WeWork raised billions from SoftBank, fueling its rapid expansion.
  - ◊ But because it **lacked profitability**, its valuation collapsed.
- ■ **Example: SpaceX (Raised Over $9 Billion, But With a Sustainable Model)**
  - ◊ Unlike WeWork, SpaceX reinvested funding into **revolutionary space technology**, leading to real revenue from NASA and commercial launches.

Lesson: VC money accelerates growth, but without a solid business model, it can lead to disaster.

5. **Visionary Leadership & Storytelling**

Unicorn founders are often **bold visionaries** who sell a compelling future.

- ■ **Example: Elon Musk (Tesla, SpaceX, Neuralink, OpenAI, Twitter/X)**
  - ◊ Musk convinces investors and the public that **his companies will change the world**.
  - ◊ This **keeps Tesla and SpaceX's valuations sky-high**, even when profits are low.
- ■ **Example: Brian Chesky (Airbnb's Vision)**
  - ◊ Instead of just pitching "home rentals," Chesky framed Airbnb as a **cultural movement**, helping it attract users and investors.

Lesson: Unicorn founders **don't just sell a product—they sell a vision.**

Case Studies: The Unicorn Path vs. The Profit Path

Let's compare two companies—one that prioritized valuation and one that focused on **profitability instead of chasing unicorn status.**

Case Study 1: Uber (The Unicorn Path – Prioritized Growth Over Profits)

- Uber raised **$25+ billion** in funding.

- Aggressively expanded into **hundreds of markets**, even at a loss.

- Prioritized **market dominance over financial sustainability.**

- **Still unprofitable** but valued at **$100+ billion.**

☞ **Uber is a prime example of a unicorn built on massive funding and rapid expansion, with profits coming later.**

Case Study 2: Basecamp (The Profit Path – Grew Without VC Money)

- Basecamp built a **profitable software business without outside investment.**

- Focused on **steady revenue growth, not hyper-scaling.**

- Still **thriving after 20+ years** but never became a unicorn.

☞ **Basecamp chose sustainable profits over chasing a billion-dollar valuation.**

Lesson: Not every successful startup needs to be a unicorn. **Some companies thrive by focusing on long-term profitability.**

The Dark Side of Chasing Unicorn Status

While reaching unicorn status is impressive, many startups **collapse under pressure.**

- **Example: Theranos (Fraud & Failure)**
  - ◊ Elizabeth Holmes raised **$700M+,** claiming to revolutionize blood testing.
  - ◊ The technology **never worked,** leading to **one of the biggest fraud scandals** in startup history.
- **Example: Quibi (Raised $1.75B, Shut Down in 6 Months)**

◊ Quibi promised to revolutionize mobile streaming.

◊ Despite **huge funding**, it **failed to attract users** and collapsed.

Lesson: A **high valuation alone doesn't guarantee success**—real business fundamentals matter.

Conclusion: Is Unicorn Status Worth Chasing?

- If your goal is **global market dominance**, **VC-backed hyper-growth** might be the right path.

- If you prefer **long-term stability and control**, prioritizing **profitability** may be the better choice.

- Some of the **biggest tech companies (Amazon, Tesla, Uber)** took years to become profitable.

In the next chapter, we'll explore **how different industries approach valuation vs. profitability—comparing tech, e-commerce, biotech, and more.**

CHAPTER 6

INDUSTRY DEEP DIVE – HOW DIFFERENT SECTORS APPROACH VALUATION VS. PROFITABILITY

Introduction: Industry Matters

A **fintech startup** and a **biotech startup** might both raise venture capital, but their approach to valuation and profitability will be completely different.

In this chapter, we'll analyze how different industries prioritize **valuation vs. profitability**, using real-world examples from **tech, e-commerce, fintech, biotech, and SaaS.**

1. **Tech Startups: Valuation First, Profitability Later**

   Why?

   - Tech startups **scale fast** with **low marginal costs** (i.e., adding new users is cheap).

   - Investors prioritize **user growth and market dominance** over short-term profitability.

   Case Study: Amazon – The Ultimate Long-Term Bet

   - For over **20 years**, Amazon **reinvested all its profits** into growth, keeping earnings close to zero.

   - Investors believed in **Jeff Bezos' vision** of building the world's largest e-commerce platform.

- Amazon is now valued at **$1.5+ trillion**, with **huge profits** from AWS (cloud computing).

☞ **Lesson:** In tech, sacrificing profits for growth can work—if you dominate the market.

2. E-Commerce: Balancing Growth & Profitability

Why?

- Unlike pure tech, e-commerce has **physical costs (inventory, logistics, warehousing).**

- Scaling requires **cash flow management**, making profitability more important.

Case Study: Shopify – The Profitable E-Commerce Giant

- Shopify scaled without **massive VC funding burns**.

- Focused on **subscription-based revenue**, ensuring profitability early.

- Now valued at **$80+ billion**, with **consistent profits**.

☞ **Lesson: E-commerce startups must balance scaling fast while keeping their unit economics sustainable.**

3. Fintech: High Valuations, But Regulation Challenges

Why?

- Fintech startups disrupt **banking, lending, investing, and payments**.

- High **user growth potential**, but **regulatory hurdles** slow down profits.

Case Study: Robinhood – Growth First, Then Profitability

- Robinhood **made stock trading free**, acquiring millions of users.

- Raised billions in funding, prioritizing **market capture over profits**.

- Faced **regulatory scrutiny** and profitability challenges, but still valued at **$10+ billion**.

☞ **Lesson: In fintech, startups must attract users first, but long-term regulatory risks can impact profits.**

4. **Biotech: Profitability is Secondary (Until a Breakthrough)**

   Why?

   - Biotech startups need **years of research, clinical trials, and regulatory approval**.

   - Profitability is **delayed**, with most companies staying in **pre-revenue mode for a decade or more**.

   Case Study: Moderna – A Biotech Unicorn That Paid Off

   - Moderna spent **years losing money** while developing mRNA technology.

   - The **COVID-19 pandemic accelerated its commercial breakthrough**.

   - Moderna's valuation jumped to **$100+ billion** when its vaccine became profitable.

☞ **Lesson: Biotech startups rely on big bets—one successful product can make up for years of losses.**

5. **SaaS (Software as a Service): The Path to Profitable Scaling**

   Why?

   - SaaS companies operate on **subscription models**, generating **predictable revenue**.

   - Scaling is **cost-effective**, making profitability easier than other industries.

   Case Study: Zoom – Profitability Without Massive Funding

   - Zoom focused on **organic growth and product quality**, avoiding heavy marketing burns.

   - Despite huge growth during COVID-19, it **remained profitable** early.

   - Now valued at **$20+ billion**, with **consistent revenues**.

☞ **Lesson: SaaS startups can scale sustainably and achieve high valuations without reckless spending.**

Comparison Table: Industry Approaches to Valuation vs. Profitability

Industry	Priority: Valuation or Profitability?	Challenges	Success Example	Failure Example
Tech (AI, Social Media, Platforms)	**Valuation First**	Market dominance, monetization delays	Amazon, Google	WeWork (overvalued, no profitability)
E-Commerce	**Balanced**	High logistics costs	Shopify, Alibaba	Wish (burned cash, collapsed)
Fintech	**Valuation First, Then Profitability**	Regulatory risks	Robinhood, Stripe	LendingClub (regulatory hurdles)
Biotech	**Valuation First (Profit Comes Late)**	Long R&D cycles	Moderna, BioNTech	Theranos (fraud, no real product)
SaaS (Software as a Service)	**Profitability Possible Early**	Competitive market	Zoom, Salesforce	Quibi (bad product-market fit)

Conclusion: Industry Strategy Matters

- **Tech & Biotech** → Prioritize valuation and funding for years before profits matter.

- **E-Commerce & Fintech** → Balance between valuation and profitability, with cash flow challenges.

- **SaaS** → Profitability is easier if growth is managed well.

In the next chapter, we'll explore **how founders can decide whether to prioritize valuation or profitability based on their business model and goals.**

Chapter 7

Decision-Making for Founders – When to Focus on Valuation vs. Profitability

Introduction: The Founder's Dilemma

Every startup founder faces a fundamental question:

- **Should I prioritize raising my company's valuation, or focus on becoming profitable?**

The right answer **depends on the business model, industry, funding strategy, and long-term vision.**

In this chapter, we'll explore:

- The key **factors** that influence a founder's decision.
- Real-life startup cases where **valuation-first** or **profit-first** strategies worked (or failed).
- A **decision-making framework** to help founders determine the best path for their startup.

Key Factors That Determine Your Startup's Path

1. **Market Size & Growth Potential**

- If your industry is **fast-growing with huge opportunities → Valuation-first may be the right strategy.**

- If your market is **niche and has limited expansion potential** → **Profitability-first makes more sense.**

Example: Google vs. Basecamp

- Google focused on **global internet dominance**, delaying profitability for years to capture the advertising market.

- Basecamp, a project management SaaS, stayed **small and profitable**, without chasing massive valuations.

Lesson: If you're in a market with **huge global potential**, prioritizing valuation can help dominate it.

2. **Industry Norms & Investor Expectations**

   - Some industries (e.g., **biotech, fintech, AI**) demand **high upfront capital**, requiring startups to **chase high valuations early**.

   - Others (e.g., **e-commerce, SaaS**) can reach **profitability sooner** and may not need aggressive fundraising.

Example: Stripe vs. Mailchimp

- **Stripe (Fintech Unicorn)** → Raised billions to scale rapidly in the **high-growth digital payments industry**.

- **Mailchimp (Bootstrapped & Profitable SaaS)** → Grew profitably without outside investment, eventually selling for **$12 billion**.

Lesson: Some industries **require VC funding to scale**, while others allow for **profitability-driven growth**.

3. **Competitive Pressure**

   - If your competitors are **raising massive funding rounds**, you may need to chase valuation to stay in the game.

   - If you have a **unique value proposition with no direct competition**, focusing on **profits early** might be a better strategy.

Example: Uber vs. Bolt

- **Uber** prioritized valuation, aggressively expanding into new markets before competitors could.

- **Bolt (a European ride-hailing company)** focused on **lean operations and early profitability**, avoiding Uber's excessive cash burn.

Lesson: If you're in a **highly competitive industry**, prioritizing valuation can help gain market share before others do.

4. **Business Model & Revenue Streams**

   - **Subscription-based businesses (e.g., SaaS, fintech)** → Profitability can come early due to recurring revenue.

   - **Marketplace businesses (e.g., Uber, Airbnb)** → Often need to prioritize valuation and scale before profitability.

Example: Netflix vs. Spotify

   - **Netflix** spent years burning cash to build a **global content library**, delaying profits.

   - **Spotify**, despite having millions of users, still struggles with **profitability due to high music licensing costs.**

Lesson: If your business requires upfront investment in technology, content, or network effects, prioritizing valuation may be necessary.

When Should Founders Focus on Valuation First?

☑ **If you're in a winner-takes-all market.**

→ If scaling fast ensures dominance (e.g., Amazon, Uber, TikTok).

☑ **If your startup has network effects.**

→ The more users join, the better your product gets (e.g., WhatsApp, Airbnb).

☑ **If your industry demands significant R&D investment.**

→ AI, biotech, and deep-tech startups need funding for years before becoming profitable.

☑ **If competition is intense and speed matters.**

→ Fintech and marketplaces often require rapid expansion to outgrow competitors.

When Should Founders Focus on Profitability First?

☑ **If you want to maintain control and ownership.**

→ Bootstrapped companies (e.g., Basecamp, Mailchimp) avoided dilution and grew sustainably.

☑ **If your business can generate revenue early.**

→ Many SaaS and e-commerce startups can become profitable within a few years.

☑ **If you're in a niche market with fewer competitors.**

→ A specialized product may not need hyper-scaling.

☑ **If investors expect short-term profitability.**

→ Some industries (e.g., e-commerce, direct-to-consumer brands) require strong cash flow management.

Decision-Making Framework: Should You Focus on Valuation or Profitability?

Use this **simple framework** to decide your startup's best path:

Question	Valuation-Focused	Profitability-Focused
Is your market large and fast-growing?	☑ Yes	✘ No
Does your business require high upfront costs (e.g., R&D, tech infrastructure)?	☑ Yes	✘ No
Do network effects play a major role in your success?	☑ Yes	✘ No
Are competitors raising significant funding?	☑ Yes	✘ No
Can you reach profitability within 3-5 years without VC money?	✘ No	☑ Yes
Do you want to maintain full ownership and control?	✘ No	☑ Yes

- **If you answered mostly ☑ in the "Valuation-Focused" column → Prioritize scaling and fundraising.**

- **If you answered mostly ☑ in the "Profitability-Focused" column → Focus on sustainable growth and cash flow.**

Case Study: Two Different Paths – Patagonia vs. Tesla

Patagonia: Profits First, Slow Growth

- Patagonia, the outdoor apparel company, **never focused on rapid scaling**.

- Grew profitably, maintained ethical sourcing, and avoided outside investors.

- Today, it's a **billion-dollar company with full founder control**.

Tesla: Valuation First, Profits Later

- Elon Musk raised billions to fund **R&D and mass production**, delaying profitability for years.

- Tesla eventually became **profitable in 2020**, but only after reaching global dominance.

- Valued at **$500+ billion**, despite lower short-term profits.

☞ **Both models worked—because they aligned with each company's vision and industry dynamics.**

Conclusion: Align Your Strategy with Your Goals

- There's **no universal answer**—choosing valuation vs. profitability depends on **market dynamics, business model, and long-term vision**.

- If you're in a **high-growth, competitive industry**, valuation-first makes sense.

- If you prefer **control and sustainable growth**, profitability-first is smarter.

- Some of the **most successful companies (Amazon, Tesla, Uber)** delayed profitability for years—but they had a clear end goal.

In the next chapter, we'll explore how investors evaluate startups—what they look for in valuation vs. profitability, and how to pitch your startup effectively.

CHAPTER 8

HOW INVESTORS THINK – VALUATION VS. PROFITABILITY IN STARTUP FUNDING

Introduction: The Investor's Perspective

For startup founders, understanding **how investors think** is critical. Venture capitalists (VCs), angel investors, and private equity firms don't just look at your product or team—they evaluate **whether your business is a good investment.**

The big question:

- **Do investors prefer high-growth startups with high valuations?**
- **Or do they favor startups that achieve profitability early?**

In this chapter, we'll explore:

- How different types of investors evaluate **valuation vs. profitability.**
- What VCs look for when funding startups.
- Why some startups raise billions despite losing money (while others struggle).
- Real-life cases of investor-backed successes and failures.

1. **How Different Investors Evaluate Startups**

    Not all investors think alike. Their priorities depend on **their risk appetite, return expectations, and investment timeline.**

1.1 **Angel Investors (Early-Stage) → Valuation First**

   ☑ Invest personal money (high-risk, high-reward).

   ☑ Want rapid growth and market dominance.

✘ Less concerned about profitability in early stages.

Example: Jeff Bezos Investing in Google (1998)

- Bezos invested **$250,000** in Google when it had no profits—just potential.

- That investment is now worth **billions**.

☞ **Angels bet on potential, not profitability.**

1.2 Venture Capitalists (VCs) → Valuation First, Profitability Later

☑ Prefer **high-growth startups** with large market opportunities.

☑ Focus on metrics like **Monthly Active Users (MAU), Annual Recurring Revenue (ARR).**

✘ Profitability is secondary unless the market is maturing.

Example: SoftBank & WeWork – A Valuation Bubble Gone Wrong

- SoftBank pumped **$10+ billion** into WeWork, believing in rapid global expansion.

- WeWork **never achieved profitability** and collapsed before its IPO.

☞ **VCs chase growth, but overvaluing a company without profits can be dangerous.**

1.3 Private Equity (PE) & Late-Stage Investors → Profitability Matters

☑ Invest in **established, profitable businesses.**

☑ Want **strong revenue, stable cash flow, and lower risk.**

✘ Less interested in risky, high-burn startups.

Example: Warren Buffett's Berkshire Hathaway – The Profit-Driven Investor

- Buffett invests in companies like **Coca-Cola, Apple, and Geico**—businesses with **strong profits and long-term stability**.

- Avoids startups with high valuations but no path to profitability.

☞ **PE firms prefer sustainable businesses over flashy valuations.**

2. What Venture Capitalists (VCs) Look for in Startups

Even if a startup isn't profitable yet, VCs don't just invest blindly. They look for:

2.1 Market Size & Growth Potential

- **Bigger markets = bigger returns** (VCs want startups that can become billion-dollar businesses).
- Example: **Facebook (Social Media = Global Market)** vs. a niche **health tech startup (small market, harder to scale).**

2.2 Revenue Growth & Unit Economics

- Investors check **Customer Acquisition Cost (CAC) vs. Lifetime Value (LTV).**
- If acquiring customers is **too expensive compared to the revenue they generate**, profitability becomes a challenge.

2.3 Network Effects & Scalability

- If more users make the platform better (e.g., **Airbnb, Uber**), VCs see long-term value.
- A company that doesn't scale well but is profitable (e.g., a **local business**) is less attractive to them.

2.4 Competitive Advantage

- Investors ask: **"What stops competitors from copying this?"**
- Example: **Tesla vs. Other EV Startups**
  - Tesla raised billions because **its battery tech and brand were unique.**
  - Many small EV startups failed because they lacked differentiation.

2.5 Exit Strategy (IPO or Acquisition?)

- VCs want **big returns,** usually through an **IPO (Initial Public Offering) or acquisition.**
- Startups that **grow fast but have no exit strategy struggle to raise money.**

3. Why Do Some Loss-Making Startups Raise Billions?

Many well-known startups raised **huge valuations without profits.** But why do investors still fund them?

Startup	Raised	Profitability?	Why Investors Backed It
Uber	$25B+	✖ No (for years)	Huge global market, network effects
Airbnb	$6B+	✖ No (initially)	Strong brand, marketplace model
Tesla	$20B+	✖ No (early on)	Tech innovation, market disruption
Snapchat	$3B+	✖ No (before IPO)	Youth user base, ad revenue potential

☞ **Investors bet on the long-term market potential, even if profits take years to materialize.**

4. **When Do Investors Start Demanding Profitability?**

- **Early-stage (Seed, Series A-B):** Profitability isn't the focus—growth is.

- **Mid-stage (Series C-D):** Investors expect signs of financial stability.

- **Late-stage (Pre-IPO):** Companies must prove they can be profitable before going public.

Example: Twitter vs. Meta (Facebook)

- **Twitter IPO'd (2013) without profits**, struggled for years, and never became a financial giant.

- **Meta (Facebook) became profitable before its IPO (2012)** and scaled into a trillion-dollar company.

☞ **Investors tolerate losses early but expect a clear path to profits in later funding rounds.**

5. **Valuation vs. Profitability: What Startups Should Focus on When Raising Money**

Stage	Best Strategy	Investor Type
Seed Stage	Valuation-first	Angel investors, Pre-seed VCs
Series A-B	Strong growth metrics, but not necessarily profitable	Venture Capitalists (VCs)
Series C-D	Signs of financial stability, reduced burn rate	Growth-stage investors
Pre-IPO	Path to profitability is crucial	Institutional investors, Hedge funds

Lesson: Startups can prioritize valuation early, but as they mature, **investors demand financial discipline.**

Conclusion: Understanding Investor Expectations is Key

- **Angel investors & VCs fund startups based on valuation and potential.**

- **Private equity & late-stage investors prefer profitability.**

- **Market size, competitive advantage, and scalability matter more than short-term profits in early stages.**

- **However, without a path to profitability, startups can collapse despite high valuations (e.g., WeWork).**

☞ **In the next chapter, we'll explore common mistakes startups make when chasing valuation or profitability—and how to avoid them.**

CHAPTER 9

THE BIGGEST MISTAKES STARTUPS MAKE – OVERVALUED & UNPROFITABLE TRAPS

Introduction: The Startup Graveyard

The startup world is full of cautionary tales—companies that raised massive valuations but failed due to **unprofitable business models, unsustainable burn rates, or investor pressure.**

In this chapter, we'll explore:

- The **most common mistakes** startups make when chasing valuation or profitability.
- Real-life cases of **overvalued companies that collapsed.**
- How **profitable startups sometimes fail** due to poor scaling decisions.
- Lessons for founders on **how to avoid these traps.**

1. **The Valuation Trap – When Startups Focus Too Much on Growth**

Some startups **chase sky-high valuations at the expense of profitability.** This often leads to **overhiring, excessive spending, and unsustainable business models.**

1.1 **The WeWork Disaster – Growth Without Profits**

- WeWork was valued at **$47 billion** despite never being profitable.
- Spent excessively on office spaces, employee perks, and marketing.
- When it trie-d to go public, investors **realized the numbers didn't add up.**
- The IPO collapsed, and its valuation plummeted to **less than $3 billion.**

☞ **Lesson:** Growth is meaningless if the unit economics don't work.

1.2 The Quibi Failure – $1.75 Billion Burned in a Year

- Quibi (a mobile streaming startup) raised **$1.75 billion** without validating its market.

- Spent aggressively on **content and ads** before proving user demand.

- **Within six months of launch, it shut down.**

☞ **Lesson:** A high valuation can't save a company without product-market fit.

1.3 Uber's Profit Struggle – Billions Raised, But Still Unprofitable

- Uber has raised **$25+ billion** since its launch.

- Despite global expansion, it still **struggles with profitability** due to high costs.

- Investors tolerated losses, but eventually, **they demand profits**.

☞ **Lesson:** Even big companies face challenges if they can't turn revenue into profit.

2. The Profitability Trap – When Startups Scale Too Slowly

While chasing profitability too early can be a strength, it can also be a **growth-limiting trap**.

2.1 The Kodak Mistake – Profitable But Ignored Innovation

- Kodak was once **one of the most profitable camera companies**.

- It had the **first digital camera prototype in 1975** but ignored it to protect its film business.

- As digital cameras took over, Kodak lost relevance and filed for bankruptcy in 2012.

☞ **Lesson:** Profitability is good, but ignoring industry trends can be fatal.

2.2 The Blockbuster Failure – Profitable, But Refused to Pivot

- Blockbuster was making **billions in profit** from DVD rentals.

- Netflix approached them with a partnership in 2000—Blockbuster laughed at the idea.

- **Netflix scaled, Blockbuster didn't.** Blockbuster collapsed in 2010.

☞ **Lesson:** A profitable business can still fail if it refuses to innovate.

2.3 Basecamp – A Profitable Company That Limited Its Scale

- Basecamp (a project management SaaS) is **highly profitable and bootstrapped**.

- But by refusing outside investment, it stayed small while competitors like **Asana and Monday.com scaled aggressively**.

☞ **Lesson:** Profitability matters, but without reinvesting in growth, competitors can overtake you.

3. The Burn Rate Problem – Spending Faster Than Revenue Grows

Many startups **burn cash at an unsustainable rate**, assuming they can always raise more funding. But when funding dries up, they collapse.

3.1 The FTX Crypto Crash – Fake Valuations & No Real Business Model

- FTX, a cryptocurrency exchange, was valued at **$32 billion**.

- Founder Sam Bankman-Fried **spent billions on marketing and sponsorships**.

- When investors looked deeper, they found **financial fraud and no real profitability**.

- FTX collapsed overnight, and Bankman-Fried was arrested.

☞ **Lesson:** A high valuation means nothing if your financials aren't solid.

3.2 Theranos – A Billion-Dollar Lie

- Theranos promised revolutionary **blood-testing technology**.

- Raised **$700 million** from investors, reaching a **$9 billion valuation**.

- The tech **never worked**, and the company collapsed in scandal.

☞ **Lesson:** Valuation hype can't replace real innovation and execution.

4. The Wrong Investor Problem – Taking Money from the Wrong People

4.1 Oyo Hotels – Investor Pressure for Growth

- Oyo, an Indian hospitality startup, raised **billions from SoftBank**.

- Investors **pushed it to expand aggressively**, leading to **bad financial decisions**.

- When the pandemic hit, Oyo **struggled to survive** because it wasn't profitable.

☞ **Lesson:** The wrong investors can push a startup into unsustainable growth.

4.2 Evernote – Too Many Investors, No Clear Focus

- Evernote raised **$300+ million** from multiple investors.

- Each investor had **different expectations** (some wanted growth, others wanted profits).

- The company **lost focus**, stagnated, and was eventually acquired for a fraction of its peak valuation.

☞ **Lesson:** The wrong investor mix can kill a startup's direction.

5. How to Avoid These Traps – Smart Growth Strategies

Here's how founders can **balance valuation and profitability** wisely:

☑ 1. Prioritize Sustainable Growth Over Hype

- Focus on **unit economics** (profit per customer).

- If customer acquisition costs are too high, **fix it before scaling**.

☑ 2. Keep Burn Rate Under Control

- Don't spend assuming **future funding will always be available**.

- Keep **at least 12-18 months of runway** to survive funding winters.

☑ 3. Pick the Right Investors

- Choose investors who align with **your long-term vision**.

- Avoid those who **force premature scaling**.

☑ 4. Adapt to Market Changes

- Companies like **Netflix pivoted from DVDs to streaming**, while Blockbuster failed to adapt.

- Stay flexible to **industry shifts and customer needs**.

☑ 5. Know When to Chase Valuation vs. Profitability

- If your market is **winner-takes-all**, valuation-first makes sense (e.g., Uber, Airbnb).

- If you're in a niche market, **profitability-first is smarter** (e.g., Basecamp, Mailchimp).

Conclusion: The Best Startups Balance Valuation & Profitability

- **Chasing valuation blindly leads to unsustainable businesses.**

- **Focusing only on profitability can limit growth and innovation.**

- **The best founders know when to shift their strategy—scaling fast when needed but keeping financial discipline.**

☞ **In the next chapter, we'll explore how to balance these two strategies in real-world execution—when to raise money, when to cut costs, and how to time profitability correctly.**

CHAPTER 10

THE ART OF BALANCING VALUATION & PROFITABILITY – A FOUNDER'S GUIDE

Introduction: Walking the Tightrope

For startups, balancing **valuation** and **profitability** is like walking a tightrope. If you lean too much toward **valuation**, you risk building a company that's all hype but no substance. If you focus solely on **profitability**, you may grow too slowly and lose market opportunities.

The best founders understand **when to prioritize each strategy** and how to make the right decisions at every stage.

In this chapter, we'll cover:

- **How to time your shift from valuation-focused to profitability-focused.**

- **Real-life case studies of startups that got it right (and those that failed).**

- **A framework for making financial decisions as a founder.**

1. **The Valuation-First vs. Profitability-First Framework**

Different startups need **different strategies** based on their industry, market conditions, and business model.

Factor	Go Valuation-First If...	Go Profitability-First If...
Market Size	Huge, high-growth market (e.g., fintech, AI, social media)	Small, niche market (e.g., B2B SaaS, consulting)
Competition	Winner-takes-all (e.g., ride-sharing, social networks)	Low competition, specialized expertise needed
Funding Availability	VC money is flowing (e.g., AI, Web3 in 2021)	Market downturn, limited VC appetite
Customer Acquisition	Requires heavy marketing spend (e.g., consumer tech)	Word-of-mouth or low-cost marketing works
Business Model	Scale now, monetize later (e.g., marketplaces, social apps)	Immediate revenue generation (e.g., subscription SaaS)

2. Case Study: Startups That Mastered the Balance

2.1 Amazon – The Ultimate Valuation-First Strategy

- Amazon **lost money for its first 7+ years** as it focused on **market domination**.

- Investors stuck with it because of its **huge market potential**.

- Once it achieved scale, it **flipped to profitability** by optimizing costs and introducing AWS (Amazon Web Services).

☞ **Lesson:** If you have long-term investor confidence, you can delay profitability to build market dominance.

2.2 Mailchimp – The Profitability-First Bootstrapped Success

- Mailchimp focused on **profitability from day one**, never raised VC funding.

- Grew steadily through **organic marketing and customer referrals**.

- Eventually sold to Intuit for **$12 billion** without ever needing external investment.

☞ **Lesson:** If your business model allows early profitability, you can grow steadily without giving up ownership.

2.3 Tesla – Smartly Transitioning from Losses to Profits

- Tesla burned cash for years, relying on **investor funding to expand production.**

- Once its **manufacturing scaled**, it became profitable and **generated billions in free cash flow.**

- The early losses were a **calculated strategy to reach dominance.**

☞ **Lesson:** Sometimes, startups must **burn cash upfront to build infrastructure**, but they need a clear path to profits.

3. The Startup Lifecycle – When to Focus on Valuation vs. Profitability

3.1 Early Stage (Seed – Series A) → *Focus on Valuation & Growth*

- ☑ Prioritize **customer acquisition and product development.**

- ☑ Investors care more about **traction, market potential, and team strength** than immediate revenue.

- ☑ It's okay to **burn cash** if you're proving demand.

Example:

- Snapchat **grew rapidly without worrying about profits**, attracting millions of users before introducing ads.

3.2 Mid-Stage (Series B – Series C) → *Shift Towards Revenue & Efficiency*

- ☑ Show strong **revenue growth**, even if not profitable yet.

- ☑ Reduce **Customer Acquisition Cost (CAC)** and improve **Lifetime Value (LTV).**

- ☑ Prove you can control costs without slowing growth.

Example:

- Uber, after years of losses, introduced **Uber Eats & Uber Freight** to diversify revenue streams.

3.3 Late-Stage (Series D – Pre-IPO) → *Profitability Becomes Crucial*

- ☑ Investors want **a clear path to profitability** before an IPO.

- ☑ Operational efficiency becomes as important as growth.

- ☑ Cut unnecessary expenses and optimize **Gross Margins.**

Example:

- Airbnb, before going public, focused on **profitability during COVID-19** by cutting marketing costs.

4. **Founder's Decision-Making Guide: When to Prioritize Valuation or Profitability**

Use this **4-step framework** to decide which approach makes sense:

Step 1: Assess Your Market Conditions

- If investors are **actively funding** your sector, growth-first makes sense.

- If funding is tight (economic downturns), **profitability-first is safer.**

Step 2: Analyze Your Business Model

- **Subscription-based SaaS?** Profitability is easier early on.

- **Social media or marketplaces?** Valuation-first is often necessary.

Step 3: Check Your Cash Runway

- If you have **12+ months of runway**, you can invest in growth.

- If you're running out of cash, shift towards **self-sustainability ASAP.**

Step 4: Align with Investor Expectations

- If your investors expect **rapid growth**, delaying profitability may be fine.

- If they demand financial stability, **proving profitability is crucial.**

5. **Common Pitfalls & How to Avoid Them**

✖ **1. Scaling Too Fast Without Sustainable Revenue**

Example: MoviePass – It offered unlimited movies for $10/month, growing fast but losing money on every customer. It collapsed.

☑ **Solution:** Ensure your **unit economics make sense** before scaling.

✖ **2. Raising Too Much Money Too Early**

Example: Fab.com – Raised $300M, burned cash on unnecessary expenses, and shut down.

☑ **Solution:** Raise only as much as you need, and **spend wisely.**

✖ **3. Delaying Profitability Indefinitely**

Example: WeWork – Focused on valuation forever without proving a sustainable business model.

☑ **Solution:** Investors will eventually demand profits—**be ready**.

✖ **4. Focusing on Profitability Too Soon & Losing Market Share**

Example: Nokia – Stuck to old models, avoided reinvestment, and lost to Apple & Samsung.

☑ **Solution:** Invest in **innovation** while maintaining financial discipline.

Conclusion: The Winning Formula for Startup Success

The best startups know when to **chase valuation** and when to **focus on profitability**.

☑ **Prioritize valuation in the early days** to attract investors & scale quickly.

☑ **Shift towards profitability** once you have a large customer base.

☑ **Never lose sight of unit economics**—scaling a broken model leads to failure.

☑ **Adapt based on market conditions**—know when investors demand profits.

☞ **In the next chapter, we'll discuss real-world strategies for founders looking to raise funding while maintaining financial discipline—how to pitch investors, negotiate valuations, and structure deals that align with long-term success.**

Chapter 11

Fundraising & Financial Discipline – A Founder's Playbook

Introduction: The Art of Raising Money Without Losing Control

Raising capital is a **double-edged sword**. On one hand, it fuels **growth, expansion, and innovation**. On the other, it can lead to **dilution, loss of control, and pressure to grow unsustainably**.

Many startups **raise too much, too soon**, while others **fail to secure enough funding** when they need it most.

In this chapter, we'll cover:

- **How to raise capital wisely without sacrificing financial discipline.**
- **How to pitch investors based on your business model.**
- **The right way to structure deals and negotiate valuations.**
- **Lessons from startups that raised money strategically vs. those that failed.**

1. **The Funding Lifecycle – When & How to Raise Capital**

1.1 **Bootstrapping vs. Fundraising – Which One Is Right for You?**

Not all startups need to raise external funding. Some can **bootstrap successfully** (self-fund through revenue), while others **need investment** to scale.

Factor	Bootstrap If...	Raise VC If...
Market Type	Niche, specialized industry (e.g., B2B SaaS, consulting)	Large, high-growth markets (e.g., AI, fintech, e-commerce)
Competition	Low competition, organic growth possible	High competition, need capital to capture market share
Revenue Model	Generates cash flow early	Requires upfront investment before revenue (e.g., marketplaces)
Founder's Goals	Wants independence & long-term profitability	Wants fast growth, possible IPO/ acquisition

☑ **Bootstrapping Example:** Mailchimp – Built profitably without VC funding, sold for **$12B to Intuit.**

☑ **VC-Backed Example:** Airbnb – Needed funding to scale globally before becoming profitable.

1.2 When to Raise Money – A Stage-by-Stage Guide

Startup Stage	Funding Needs	Investor Expectations	Example Startups
Pre-Seed (Idea Stage)	Small capital for product development & validation	Clear problem-solving idea, MVP	Figma, Superhuman
Seed (Early Traction)	Build first version, test product-market fit	Some revenue traction, early users	Stripe, Robinhood
Series A (Scaling Up)	Expand customer base, improve tech	Revenue growth, strong retention	Notion, Duolingo
Series B & Beyond	Market dominance, international growth	Clear path to profitability	Uber, Airbnb

🖋 **Key Insight:** The later the stage, the more investors care about **revenue, margins, and financial discipline** rather than just growth.

2. How to Pitch Investors Based on Your Business Model

Investors look for different things based on **what kind of startup you're running.**

2.1 Venture-Backed Model – Sell the Vision, Show Growth Potential

For high-growth startups (e.g., fintech, AI, marketplaces), investors care about:

- ☑ **Market size** – Can this become a $1B+ company?
- ☑ **Revenue potential** – Can you 10x revenue in 3-5 years?
- ☑ **Team strength** – Can the founders execute the vision?
- ☑ **Scalability** – Can the business grow without excessive costs?

Example: Stripe raised $2M in seed funding by showing how online payments were broken and how they would fix it.

2.2 Profitability-First Model – Show Strong Unit Economics

For bootstrapped or profitable startups (e.g., SaaS, e-commerce), investors care about:

- ☑ **Revenue & margins** – Is there a clear path to long-term profitability?
- ☑ **Customer retention** – Do users stay & pay over time?
- ☑ **Cost efficiency** – Can you grow without excessive spending?

Example: Basecamp never took VC money because they proved they could **acquire and retain customers profitably.**

3. Smart Fundraising Strategies – How to Get the Best Deal

3.1 The Right Way to Set Valuation – Avoid Overpricing Yourself

Overvaluation can lead to **unrealistic expectations, pressure from investors, and potential down rounds later.**

⊞ **Case Study: WeWork's Valuation Disaster**

- At its peak, WeWork was valued at **$47B** despite massive losses.
- When it tried to go public, investors **saw the financials didn't add up.**
- The IPO collapsed, and its valuation dropped to **less than $3B.**

- ☑ **Lesson:** Set a valuation that reflects **realistic growth and financial fundamentals.**

3.2 Avoiding Dilution – How to Retain Control

If you raise **too much money too early**, you may lose control of your company.

💡 **Example: Zuckerberg's Smart Fundraising Strategy**

- Facebook raised funding **strategically** while ensuring **Zuckerberg kept control.**
- By the time Facebook went public, he still owned **more than 50% voting power.**

How to Protect Yourself:

- Raise only **as much as needed** at each stage.
- Negotiate for **founder-friendly terms** (e.g., dual-class shares).

3.3 Choosing the Right Investors – Not All Money Is Good Money

Investors come with **different expectations**—some push for **aggressive growth**, others prefer **steady scaling.**

⏱ **SoftBank's Impact on Startups (Oyo, WeWork, etc.)**

- SoftBank gave startups **huge funding rounds**, forcing them to **expand too fast.**
- Many struggled when they couldn't meet unrealistic growth targets.

☑ **Best Approach:**

- Choose investors who align with your **long-term vision.**
- Look for **strategic investors** who provide mentorship, not just money.

4. Maintaining Financial Discipline After Raising Money

4.1 Avoiding the "Burn Rate Trap" – Spend Smartly

Many startups fail because they **burn through cash too fast** without hitting key milestones.

⚰ **Example: Quibi – Burned \$1.75B in a Year & Shut Down**

- Spent millions on marketing before proving product-market fit.
- Couldn't acquire enough users and shut down within 6 months.

☑ **Lesson:** Raise what you need, but **spend it wisely.**

4.2 Managing Costs Without Killing Growth

How to stay lean while scaling:

✓ **Hire only when necessary** – Avoid overstaffing too early.

✓ **Automate processes** – Reduce operational costs.

✓ **Monitor unit economics** – If CAC (customer acquisition cost) is too high, **fix it before scaling**.

▦ **Example: Airbnb's Cost Optimization During COVID-19**

- Cut unnecessary marketing expenses while **maintaining core operations**.

- Became profitable by focusing on **high-margin revenue streams**.

5. Key Takeaways: How to Raise Money Without Losing Control

☑ **1. Choose the right funding path** – Not every startup needs VC money.

☑ **2. Raise money in stages** – Don't take too much too soon.

☑ **3. Set realistic valuations** – Overpricing can lead to problems later.

☑ **4. Spend wisely** – Avoid unnecessary expenses & optimize costs.

☑ **5. Pick the right investors** – Not all money is good money.

Conclusion: Raising Money is a Means, Not an End

Startups don't succeed just because they **raise millions**—they succeed because they **build great businesses**.

- Raising funds should be **a tool for growth, not a goal itself**.

- Financial discipline is **just as important as raising capital**.

- The best startups **balance valuation, profitability, and sustainable growth**.

☞ **In the next chapter, we'll dive into how startups can prepare for IPOs or exits—when to go public, when to sell, and how to maximize value for founders and investors.**

CHAPTER 12

IPOs, Acquisitions & Exit Strategies – When & How to Cash Out

Introduction: The Founder's Endgame

Every startup eventually faces a **pivotal decision**:

- **Go public (IPO)** and scale as a publicly traded company?

- **Sell the company (acquisition or merger)** for a lucrative exit?

- **Stay private and keep growing** without external pressure?

The right **exit strategy** depends on your startup's **growth, market conditions, and investor expectations**.

In this chapter, we'll explore:

- **The pros and cons of IPOs vs. acquisitions.**

- **Real-life case studies of startups that exited successfully—and those that failed.**

- **A decision-making framework for founders evaluating exit options.**

1. **The Three Exit Paths for Startups**

1.1 **Initial Public Offering (IPO) – Going Public**

An IPO means your startup **sells shares to the public** on a stock exchange, raising capital for future growth.

☑ **Advantages:**

- Access to **large-scale funding** for expansion.

- Increased **brand credibility** and trust.
- Investors & employees can **cash out their shares**.

✖ **Disadvantages:**

- **Regulatory pressure** (SEC rules, financial disclosures).
- Short-term **stock market fluctuations** affect company decisions.
- Public companies face **shareholder pressure** for quarterly profits.

🖾 **Example: Airbnb's Smart IPO Strategy**

- Delayed its IPO until **2020** to **prove profitability**.
- Focused on **cost-cutting & efficiency** during COVID-19.
- Had a **successful IPO at a $100B valuation**, exceeding expectations.

1.2 Acquisition – Selling to a Bigger Company

A startup is **acquired by a larger firm** for a strategic reason—technology, talent, or market expansion.

☑ **Advantages:**

- **Immediate financial reward** for founders & investors.
- No need to deal with **public market volatility**.
- Access to the acquirer's **resources & customer base**.

✖ **Disadvantages:**

- **Loss of independence**—the acquiring company may change strategy.
- Potential for **culture clashes** and layoffs.
- Not always **maximizing valuation** compared to IPO.

⏱ **Example: Instagram's $1B Acquisition by Facebook**

- Instagram had **only 13 employees** and zero revenue in 2012.
- Facebook acquired it for **$1 billion**, betting on future growth.
- Today, Instagram generates **$32B+ in annual revenue**—some argue it was undervalued.

1.3 Staying Private – The Long-Term Growth Approach

Some startups choose to **stay private**, rejecting IPOs and acquisitions to focus on **sustainable growth**.

☑ **Advantages:**

- Avoids **stock market volatility & shareholder pressure**.
- Founders retain **full control** over decision-making.
- Can reinvest profits into **long-term innovation**.

✖ **Disadvantages:**

- Limited access to **large-scale capital**.
- Investors & employees have **fewer options to cash out**.
- Can face pressure from **early investors seeking returns**.

🔍 **Example: Patagonia – Staying Private for Mission-Driven Growth**

- Refused to go public, ensuring **long-term sustainability focus**.
- Profits reinvested in **climate initiatives** instead of shareholders.
- **Founder Yvon Chouinard transferred ownership to a trust** to maintain its mission.

2. IPO vs. Acquisition – How to Decide?

2.1 Key Factors to Consider

Factor	Go Public (IPO)	Sell (Acquisition)
Growth Potential	High long-term revenue growth expected	Market is slowing, better to exit early
Independence	Want to remain in control	Willing to integrate into a larger company
Market Conditions	Favorable public market (high valuations)	IPO market is weak, but acquirer is offering a strong deal
Investor Pressure	Need to give VC investors an exit	Investors prefer a quick and profitable sale

📊 **Case Study: LinkedIn's IPO vs. Twitter's Acquisition**

- LinkedIn went public in **2011**, but struggled with **Wall Street pressure**.
- Microsoft acquired LinkedIn for **$26B in 2016**, offering stability & resources.
- Twitter initially IPO'd but was later acquired by Elon Musk for **$44B in 2022**.

☑ **Lesson:** Sometimes **an acquisition is the better long-term play** than staying public.

3. **Common Mistakes & How to Avoid Them**

✖ **1. Rushing to IPO Without a Profitable Model**

Example: WeWork's IPO Disaster (2019)

- Filed for an IPO with **huge losses & no path to profitability**.
- Investors rejected its **overhyped valuation** ($47B → $3B crash).
- The IPO was canceled, and CEO Adam Neumann was forced out.

☑ **Solution:** Prove sustainable **revenue & profit potential** before going public.

✖ **2. Selling Too Early & Undervaluing the Business**

Example: YouTube's $1.65B Sale to Google (2006)

- YouTube sold early despite **massive future potential**.
- Today, it generates **$40B+ per year** for Google.
- Founders could have held on for a much larger exit.

☑ **Solution:** Consider long-term growth before accepting a buyout.

✖ **3. Mismanaging an Acquisition Integration**

Example: Yahoo's Failed $3.6B Acquisition of Tumblr (2013)

- Bought Tumblr but **failed to monetize or integrate it well**.
- Sold Tumblr for **less than $3M in 2019**, a **99% value loss**.

☑ **Solution:** Ensure cultural & strategic alignment before selling.

4. **The Founder's Decision Framework – When & How to Exit**

Use this **5-step framework** to make the right exit decision:

Step 1: Assess Your Growth Trajectory

- Are you growing fast enough to justify an IPO?
- Would an acquirer **accelerate your success**?

Step 2: Evaluate Market Conditions

- Are public markets valuing similar companies highly?
- Are strategic buyers actively acquiring startups?

Step 3: Consider Investor & Employee Expectations

- Do your early investors need liquidity?
- Will employees benefit from an IPO or stock sale?

Step 4: Determine Your Risk Tolerance

- IPOs bring **higher risks but potential long-term gains**.
- Acquisitions provide **security but limit future upside**.

Step 5: Seek Strategic Advice

- Consult **financial advisors & experienced entrepreneurs** before deciding.

5. Key Takeaways: Maximizing Your Exit Strategy

- ☑ 1. **Timing is everything** – Don't rush into an IPO or acquisition without strong fundamentals.
- ☑ 2. **Evaluate long-term value** – The highest offer isn't always the best decision.
- ☑ 3. **Protect your company's culture & mission** – Avoid acquisitions that will disrupt your team.
- ☑ 4. **Be prepared for due diligence** – Buyers & investors will scrutinize your **financials, team, and business model**.
- ☑ 5. **Think beyond the exit** – What will you do after selling or going public?

Conclusion: The Exit is Just the Beginning

Exiting a startup isn't just about **cashing out**—it's about setting up the business for its **next phase of growth**.

Whether you choose an **IPO, acquisition, or staying private**, the best founders ensure their companies **continue to thrive beyond their leadership**.

☞ **In the final chapter, we'll explore post-exit strategies—what happens after a successful IPO or sale, and how founders can transition to their next big venture.**

Chapter 13

Life After the Exit – What's Next for Founders?

Introduction: The Post-Exit Dilemma

For many founders, an exit—whether through **an IPO, acquisition, or another liquidity event**—marks the **culmination of years of effort, sacrifices, and hard work.**

But after the celebrations, the big question arises: **What's next?**

Some founders struggle with **losing purpose**, while others **jump straight into a new venture.**

In this chapter, we'll explore:

- How founders navigate life after an exit.
- **What happens when they stay vs. leave after an acquisition or IPO.**
- **Strategies for wealth management and reinvestment.**
- **Real-life case studies of founders who thrived—or struggled—post-exit.**

1. **Staying or Leaving After an Exit – The Founder's Choice**

   When a startup **goes public or gets acquired**, founders often face a **critical decision:**

   1. **Stay & continue leading** the company under new ownership.
   2. **Leave & start fresh**, either launching a new venture or retiring.

1.1 **Staying After an IPO or Acquisition**

   Many founders choose to **stay post-exit** to ensure the company's long-term success.

☑ **Advantages:**

- Provides **continuity & leadership stability**.
- Allows founders to **shape the company's future**.
- Helps maintain the **company culture & mission**.

✕ **Disadvantages:**

- Increased **bureaucracy & investor pressure**.
- Less **autonomy**—decisions now involve shareholders or acquirers.
- Potential **loss of motivation** once personal financial goals are met.

🀫 **Example: Brian Chesky (Airbnb) – Staying Post-IPO**

- Despite Airbnb's **$100B IPO**, CEO Brian Chesky stayed.
- Focused on **long-term brand building & innovation**.
- Maintains a **vision-driven leadership approach**, ensuring Airbnb evolves.

1.2 Leaving to Start a New Chapter

Some founders choose to **step away post-exit**, either to **launch a new startup, invest, or focus on philanthropy**.

☑ **Advantages:**

- Freedom to **pursue new ideas** without corporate constraints.
- Ability to **invest in & mentor new entrepreneurs**.
- Can take time for **personal growth, family, or passion projects**.

✕ **Disadvantages:**

- Risk of **losing identity & purpose** after leaving.
- May regret **giving up control too soon**.
- Starting fresh can be **emotionally & financially draining**.

💡 **Example: Kevin Systrom & Mike Krieger (Instagram) – Leaving After an Acquisition**

- Sold Instagram to Facebook for **$1B in 2012**.
- Stayed for **six years**, then left due to **conflicts with Mark Zuckerberg**.

- Later launched **Artifact (AI-powered news platform)**, continuing their entrepreneurial journey.

2. **Managing Wealth & Investments Post-Exit**

A **big exit** often leads to **sudden wealth**, which can be a blessing or a burden.

2.1 Smart Financial Management Strategies

Founders need a **wealth strategy** to avoid common pitfalls like:

✘ **Overspending & bad investments.**

✘ **Losing focus on long-term goals.**

✘ **Failing to diversify assets.**

☑ **Wealth Allocation Framework (Example for a $50M Exit)**

Asset Class	Allocation %	Why It Matters
Diversified Stock Portfolio	30%	Stable long-term growth
Real Estate	20%	Passive income & appreciation
Private Equity & VC	20%	Investing in new startups
Philanthropy & Impact Funds	10%	Giving back to society
Personal Ventures & Passion Projects	10%	Funding new businesses
Cash & Liquidity	10%	Safety & flexibility

⏱ **Example: Jeff Bezos – Amazon to Space Ventures**

- After stepping down as Amazon's CEO, he invested in **Blue Origin (space tech).**
- Pours billions into **climate initiatives & philanthropy.**
- Maintains **a diverse wealth portfolio**, including media (Washington Post).

3. Becoming an Investor or Mentor – Giving Back to Startups

3.1 Angel Investing – Funding the Next Generation

Many exited founders become **angel investors**, using their wealth & experience to **support new startups.**

☑ **Why Become an Angel Investor?**

- Stay involved in **innovation & entrepreneurship**.
- Mentor young founders & **avoid their mistakes**.
- Potential for **high financial returns** on new ventures.

📊 **Example: Naval Ravikant – Founder to Super Angel**

- Co-founded **AngelList** after exiting his first company.
- Became an **early investor in Uber, Twitter, and Notion**.
- Now focuses on **mentorship, philosophy, & startup investing**.

3.2 Joining a Venture Capital Firm

Some founders **join or start their own VC firm** to make larger investments.

💡 **Example: Marc Andreessen – From Netscape to Andreessen Horowitz (A16Z)**

- Co-founded **Netscape**, one of the first web browsers.
- After its exit, he launched **A16Z**, a top VC firm investing in **Airbnb, Coinbase, OpenAI**.

☑ **Why Become a VC?**

- Invest in **high-growth startups**.
- Guide & mentor new entrepreneurs.
- Stay connected to the **startup ecosystem**.

4. The Psychological Shift – Finding a New Purpose

Many founders **struggle with identity loss** after selling their startup.

✖ **Common Emotional Challenges Post-Exit**

1. **Lack of Direction** – "What do I do now?"
2. **Fear of Irrelevance** – No longer at the center of the tech world.
3. **Struggles with Boredom** – Used to high-energy startup life.

☑ **Ways to Overcome It:**

- **Build new ventures** – Stay creative & challenge yourself.
- **Engage in philanthropy** – Find purpose beyond money.
- **Teach & mentor** – Share knowledge with the next generation.

🌐 **Example: Bill Gates – Tech to Global Impact**

- After Microsoft, shifted focus to **global health & philanthropy**.
- Gates Foundation has donated **$50B+ to social causes**.
- Found a **new purpose beyond business success**.

5. Key Takeaways: Thriving After the Exit

1. ☑ **Choose wisely** – Decide whether to stay or leave post-exit.
2. ☑ **Manage wealth smartly** – Diversify investments & avoid reckless spending.
3. ☑ **Invest in the startup ecosystem** – Angel investing & mentoring keep you engaged.
4. ☑ **Find new purpose** – Start a passion project, charity, or new business.
5. ☑ **Think beyond money** – The best legacies are built on impact, not just wealth.

Conclusion: The Exit is Just Another Beginning

An exit is not **the end of a founder's journey—it's a transition to new opportunities**.

The best founders **reinvent themselves**, whether through **new startups, investing, philanthropy, or mentorship**.

☞ **Final Thought:** What you do **after the exit** defines your legacy more than the exit itself.

Final Words – Thank You for Reading!

This concludes our book on valuation vs. profitability for startups.

We've explored:

- ✓ How to balance **growth & financial sustainability**.
- ✓ Real-world startup stories of **successes & failures**.
- ✓ Strategies for **fundraising, scaling, exiting, and beyond**.

🚀 **Now, it's your turn.**

Whether you're building, scaling, or exiting—**make your startup journey count!**

THE STARTUP JOURNEY – PROFITABILITY, VALUATION & LEGACY

The Founder's Dilemma: Profitability vs. Valuation

Throughout this book, we've explored one of the most critical decisions every startup founder faces:

Should you focus on increasing valuation or building profitability?

There is no **one-size-fits-all** answer. Some of the world's most successful startups scaled through aggressive **valuation-driven growth**, while others prioritized **profitability from day one**.

The right choice depends on:

- **Your business model & industry** (Tech vs. Traditional industries).
- **Market conditions & investor expectations.**
- **Your long-term vision as a founder.**

Key Lessons from This Book

1. **Profitability & Valuation Are Not Mutually Exclusive**
   - The most sustainable startups **balance both valuation & profitability.**
   - Even high-growth companies like **Airbnb & Amazon eventually prioritized profitability.**

📌 **Lesson:** Growth at all costs isn't always the answer. If you ignore profitability too long, you might not survive.

2. **Timing is Everything**

    - **There's a time to raise money & a time to cut costs.**

    - Startups that scale **too quickly without a solid foundation** often fail (e.g., WeWork).

    - Startups that **focus too much on profits too early** might miss out on market opportunities.

✍ **Lesson: The best founders adapt their strategy based on where their startup is in its lifecycle.**

3. **Fundraising is a Means, Not an End**

    - Raising VC funding **doesn't equal success**—it's just a tool for growth.

    - Many great companies (e.g., **Mailchimp**) bootstrapped & scaled **without venture capital**.

    - Some startups **burned through VC money & collapsed** because they didn't have a real business model.

✍ **Lesson:** Raise funding only when necessary, and ensure it fuels **real business growth**—not just vanity metrics.

4. **Scaling Smart is More Important Than Scaling Fast**

    - **Blitzscaling (hypergrowth)** works for some (Uber, Amazon) but destroys others (Quibi, Fast).

    - **Sustainable scaling** ensures that the business can withstand market downturns.

✍ **Lesson:** Scale at a **pace that matches your business fundamentals**—not just investor expectations.

5. **A Great Exit is About More Than Money**

    - IPOs & acquisitions **aren't always the best path**—some companies thrive by staying private.

    - Founders who **sell too early** often regret it, while those who stay too long might miss exit opportunities.

    - The best founders **think beyond the exit** and focus on **impact, culture, and long-term legacy**.

🏷 **Lesson:** Your startup's exit should align with your **personal goals & vision**, not just financial gain.

The Founder's Final Choice: What Kind of Startup Are You Building?

As a founder, you **own your startup's narrative**.

You can **chase valuation** and build the next billion-dollar unicorn.

Or you can **prioritize profitability** and build a long-lasting, self-sustaining business.

Some of the world's greatest companies—**Amazon, Google, Tesla**—pursued valuation-first strategies before becoming highly profitable.

Others—**Mailchimp, Basecamp, Patagonia**—chose **profitability-first** and created long-term, sustainable businesses.

What kind of startup will you build?

That's the real question.

Whatever path you choose, make sure:

- ✓ **Your business model is strong.**
- ✓ **You understand when to prioritize valuation vs. profitability.**
- ✓ **You stay adaptable in a constantly changing market.**
- ✓ **You build a company that aligns with your vision & values.**

Final Words: Your Journey Starts Now

This book was written **to help founders make smarter decisions** about growth, funding, scaling, and exiting.

🚀 **Now it's your turn to take action.**

Whether you're:

- **Launching a new startup**
- **Scaling & fundraising**
- **Planning your exit strategy**

Make your choices **strategically, not emotionally.**

The best startups are built by founders who **understand the balance between valuation and profitability**—and know when to focus on each.

Wishing you success on your startup journey!